PSALM 121

I look to the mountains:
where will my help come from?
My help will come from the LORD,
who made heaven and earth.

He will not let you fail:
your protector is always awake.
The protector of Israel
never dozes or sleeps.

The LORD will guard you:
he is by your side
to protect you.

The sun will not hurt you during the day,
nor the moon during the night.
The LORD will protect you from all danger:
he will keep you safe.
He will protect you as you come and go,
now and forever.

(Psalm 121 from the Good News Bible.)

EMPTINESS

LORD,
I am numb; my heart is heavy with grief.
There is this dull ache in me,
this feeling of being empty, dried out,
crushed.

Around me, there is only emptiness,
a great abyss that draws me in
and engulfs me.
Wherever I go, I find no rest.
I search in vain
there is no one...
For me, there is nothing but loneliness.

Where are you, LORD?
How will you help me,
O LORD?
My pain is so great...
You, at least, do not abandon me:
You are my GOD.

(Psalm 142:7
Set me free from my distress, so that I may praise your name.)

SOLITUDE

O LORD, MY GOD!
I never could have imagined
that this would happen
to me.

I loved him (her) so.
But death took him (her) from me,
took him (her) forever...
We could have done
so much more together;
we had so much more to share...
And now, what am I left with?
No one... Nothing.
No, I cannot believe it.
LORD, let it not be so!

Help me, O LORD.
This loneliness is crushing me.
I cannot bear so much sorrow.

(Psalm 141:1 - I call upon you, LORD; make haste to me!
Give ear to my voice when I call to you!)

WITHDRAWAL

MY GOD,
How awful!
I loved him (her), but even so,
his (her) life has ended.

Nothing, no one
will ever fill the void
that I feel deep within me.
We will never talk together again.
So many things have been left unsaid,
unfinished...
I wish I could vanish completely,
lock windows and doors,
hide in the dark,
so as not to see anything,
or hear anything:
lock myself in my solitude
to find him (her) again.

But I know
it cannot be,
that it will never
LORD, help me!

(1 Thessalonians 4:14 - For if we believe that Jesus died and rose again,
even so, through Jesus, God will bring with him those who have fallen asleep.)

STAY WITH ME

Yes, LORD,
I know...
but I don't want to believe it yet.

We were so close
and now, it is all over...
I have so many things to settle today,
but little by little,
I am beginning to understand better...
Help me, LORD,
to live through this terrible ordeal.
Give me courage
when I need it.
Help me to meet people
who will understand my frailty
and my tears.
Dear GOD,
stay with me,
share my sorrow.

(Psalm 138:7 - When I am surrounded by troubles, you keep me safe.)

PULLING THROUGH

LORD, I want to pull through:
I must pull myself out
of this dark sorrow.
I cannot live constantly depressed.
I have no right to let myself go:
It serves no purpose,
neither for those who stay behind
nor for those who have left:
no, it helps no one!
But you, dear GOD,
help me to be myself again,
gradually...
Teach me to live again.
Let me recognize
those who are ready to help me.
I need to hear encouraging words,
to hold a friendly hand.
I am waiting for the ray of sunlight
that will warm me,
for the blue of the sky
that will give me again a bit of hope.
LORD, stay with me.

(Psalm 109:21 - Lord, help me as you have promised, and rescue me
because of the goodness of your love.)

LIFT THE WEIGHT

DEAR GOD,
I am slowly
rediscovering life.
I realize that there are
so many beautiful things
in this world in which I am still living.
I see flowers blooming,
I hear birds singing in the morning.
And mostly, I know there are people
who wish me well.
LORD, open my eyes,
my ears and my heart!
Dry my tears,
so none will have been shed in vain!
Each one is precious to you,
and all are precious to the loved one I have lost.
Do not let me become hardened.
Lift the weight from my heart.
Whatever happens, I know you will be faithful to me,
You, my LORD and my GOD!

(Romans 14:7-9 - None of us lives for himself only and none of us dies
for himself only. If we live, it is for the Lord that we live, and if we die,
it is for the Lord that we die. So then, whether we live or whether we die,
we are the Lord's. For to this end Christ died and lived again,
that he might be Lord both of the dead and of the living.)

TEACH ME TO LIVE

DEAR GOD,
we shared so many happy moments
when we were together:
so many wonderful days
during all those years...

I feel sorrow
when I think of my loss;
but no one can take away from me
the memory of all those happy moments.
Now, this treasure of great value
will be with me all my life,
bringing me joy,
but also pain, sometimes...
LORD, don't permit
the pain to overwhelm me!
Let me also take care of myself.

LORD,
help me understand
that life goes on,
that, after all,
there is still beauty in my life!

(Wisdom 1:13-14 - God did not invent death, and he does not delight in the
death of the living. For he created all things that they might exist.)

NEW MEANING TO LIFE

DEAR GOD,
the pain of our parting still grips me,
although I know I have not travelled this road in vain.

I have become more sensitive to others,
and capable of compassion.
My eyes and my ears have opened:
I am more aware of all the misery in the world.
I am no longer indifferent to
hunger and human suffering.
I am concerned
and, with my limited means,
I want to do something
wherever I may be.

Thank you, LORD,
for all this.
Through you,
my life now has new meaning.

(Matthew 11:28-30 - Come to me, all you who labor and are heavy laden and
I will give you rest. Take my yoke upon you, and learn from me; for I am gentle
and lowly in heart, and you will find rest for your souls. For my yoke is easy
and my burden light.)

REUNITED

Luke 17:20-21 - The kingdom of God is not coming with signs to be observed: nor will they say, "Look, here it is!" or "There it is!" For behold, the kingdom of God is in the midst of you.)